THE JUNGLE CREW

mibo®

Button
BOOKS

MADELEINE ROGERS

Inside the leafy jungle,
in the dappled light,
there's endless mischief going on
throughout the day and night.

The canopies are quivering,
there's rustling in the trees.

Swinging, jumping, playing;
it's a troop of chimpanzees.

Macaws just shout instead of sing,
a yappy screeching sound.

Their colored feathers catch
the sunlight as they fly around.

If you can spy a tiger's eye you are probably too near.

In case he's feeling hungry,
it's best to COME BACK HERE!

Toucans live in holes in trees.
Can you see some here?

They use their beaks to reach sweet fruit that grows throughout the year.

Tree frogs love to live high up,
so are careful when they *hop*.

They lay their eggs near water;
ready… set… drop!

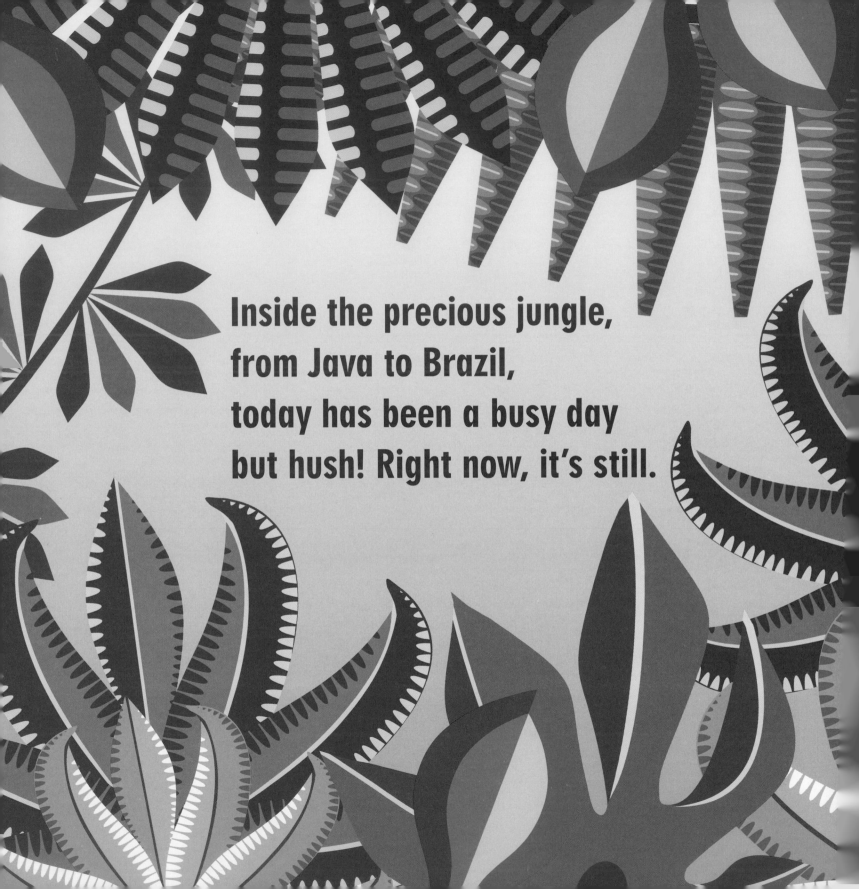

Inside the precious jungle,
from Java to Brazil,
today has been a busy day
but hush! Right now, it's still.

First published 2015 by Button Books, an imprint of Guild of Master Craftsman Publications Ltd, Castle Place, 166 High Street, Lewes, East Sussex BN7 1XU, UK. Text, designs, and illustrations © Madeleine Rogers, 2015. Copyright in the Work © GMC Publications Ltd, 2015. ISBN 978 1 90898 532 3. Distributed by Publishers Group West in the United States. All rights reserved. The right of Madeleine Rogers to be identified as the author of this work has been asserted in accordance with the Copyright, Designs, and Patents Act 1988, sections 77 and 78. No part of this publication may be reproduced, stored in a retrieval system, or transmitted in any form or by any means without the prior permission of the publisher and copyright owner. This book is sold subject to the condition that all designs are copyright and are not for commercial reproduction without the permission of the designer and copyright owner. Whilst every effort has been made to obtain permission from the copyright holders for all material used in this book, the publishers will be pleased to hear from anyone who has not been appropriately acknowledged and to make the correction in future reprints. The publishers and author can accept no legal responsibility for any consequences arising from the application of information, advice, or instructions given in this publication. A catalog record for this book is available from the British Library. Color origination by GMC Reprographics. Printed in China.

Button BOOKS

FSC
www.fsc.org
MIX
Paper from
responsible sources
FSC® C020056